Morphy Richards
Slow Cooker
Cookbook UK 2023

Katie Craig

Contents

SOUPS & STEWS RECIPES 53

APPETIZERS RECIPES 61

SNACK RECIPES 69

SIDE DISH RECIPES 76

VEGETABLE & VEGETARIAN RECIPES 83

OTHER SLOW COOKER RECIPES 90

INTRODUCTION
How a slow cooker works

A slow cooker is a great cooking method for someone who's busy and wants to prepare easy meals without having to spend a lot of time in the kitchen. It's the "set it and forget it" kind of meal preparation method that cooks your food for multiple hours, hence the name "slow cooker."

Most slow cookers have timers that allow for a meal to be slow cooked throughout the day — but not overcooked — and then switched to a "warm" setting so the food remains hot and safe to eat. To maximize the taste and texture of your meal and to avoid overcooking, it's important to follow the indicated cooking times on the recipe you're following. But, if you get delayed for an hour or so, your slow cooker meal is probably okay for a couple of hours if it defaults to the warm setting once it is finished cooking.

Not every slow cooker recipe is equally healthy

Like every cooking method, there's almost always a way to make a meal that trends toward unhealthy — slow cooker cooking included.

When scanning a slow cooker recipe, watch out for too many:

» High-fat ingredients, such as cream-based soups, cream cheese and butter

» High-sodium ingredients, such as canned vegetables, broths, soups or beans

» High-carb, low-veggie ingredient lists, such as pastas or casserole-like dishes

In addition, if you choose a slow cooker recipe that's meat-heavy, such as pulled pork, be sure to have plenty of veggies as a side to complete your well-balanced meal.

The good news, however, is that — with a little planning — almost any recipe can be modified to reduce its fat, sodium, sugar or carbohydrate content.

Ingredient substitutions that can make any slow cooker recipe healthier

If you stumble on a slow cooker recipe you want to try, but it contains some of the unhealthier ingredients above, you can almost always make some healthier substitutions!

Here are some substitutions and other ideas to help boost the healthfulness of your slow cooker dish:

» Choose whole-grain options over refined carbohydrates. For instance, swap white pasta with whole-grain pasta or beans. Whole-grain choices add both fiber and protein to your dish.

» Rinse and drain canned vegetables and beans. Canned items are typically high in sodium, and draining the liquid can help lower the sodium content.

» Replace mayonnaise with Greek yogurt. Given their similar textures and cooking behaviors, this swap gives you less fat and more protein.

» Cut the cheese. Many recipes call for multiple cups of cheese, but you can typically cut this amount, and therefore the fat (and sodium) content, by half.

» More herbs, less salt. To help pack a flavorful punch while staying healthy, opt for fresh or dried herbs instead of more salt.

Some final slow cooker tips (just in case you need 'em)

Cooking with a new kitchen gadget can be intimidating, but here are a few tips if you're just getting started.

1. Avoid "The Danger Zone"

It's important to make sure your food doesn't enter the temperature range where bacteria can grow, which falls between 40 and 140 degrees Fahrenheit. Generally, most slow cookers can hold a temperature on the warm setting between 145 and 165 degrees Fahrenheit for two to four hours (check your slow cooker manual for your model's specifications). But, I always err on the side of caution, only keeping food on the warm setting (after it's fully cooked) for two hours at most. I also recommend checking the food's internal temperature with a food thermometer to make sure it's thoroughly cooked.

2. Preheat your slow cooker

Just like when you're using an oven, you don't want raw food to spend a lot of time in "The Danger Zone" as your cooker starts the process of coming up to temperature. Instead of just throwing everything in and then pressing "Start," you'll want to preheat your slow cooker. In addition, if your meat is frozen, make sure it's safely thawed before adding to your slow cooker.

3. Your slow cooker can't cook on "Warm"

Don't attempt to cook meat on the "Warm" setting — it won't get hot enough. It's also a good idea to keep the lid on as much as possible in order to not only retain heat, but also moisture.

BREAKFAST RECIPES

Sausage Bake

Ingredients:

- 1 C. potato, grated
- ½ white onion, minced
- 1-lb. smoked andouille sausage, sliced
- 1 C. cheddar cheese, shredded
- ½ C. heavy cream
- 1 tsp. sesame oil

Servings: 5

Cooking Time: 8 Hours

Directions:

1. In the bowl mix grated potato, onion, smoked sausages, cheese, and heavy cream.
2. Then brush the Slow Cooker with sesame oil.
3. Put the sausage mixture in the Slow Cooker.
4. Close the lid and cook the bake on Low for 8 hours.

Cowboy Breakfast Casserole

Ingredients:

- 1-lb. ground beef
- 5 eggs, beaten
- 1 C. grass-fed Monterey Jack cheese, shredded
- Salt and pepper to taste
- 1 avocado, peeled and diced
- A handful of cilantro, chopped
- A dash of hot sauce

Servings: 6

Cooking Time: 3 Hours

Directions:

1. In a skillet over medium flame, sauté the beef for three minutes until slightly golden.
2. Pour into the Slow Cooker and pour in eggs.
3. Sprinkle with cheese on top and season with salt and pepper to taste.
4. Close the lid and cook on high for 4 hours or on low for 6 hours.
5. Serve with avocado, cilantro and hot sauce.

Chocolate Quinoa

Ingredients:

- 1 C. quinoa
- 1 C. coconut milk
- 1 C. milk
- 2 tbsp. cocoa powder
- 3 tbsp. maple syrup
- 4 dark chocolate squares, chopped

Servings: 4
Cooking Time: 6 Hours

Directions:

1. In your Slow Cooker, mix quinoa with coconut milk, milk, cocoa powder, maple syrup and chocolate, stir, cover and cook on Low for 6 hours.
2. Stir quinoa mix again, divide into bowls and serve.

Broccoli Quiche

Ingredients:

- 2 tbsp. oatmeal
- 1 C. broccoli, chopped
- ½ C. fresh cilantro, chopped
- ¼ C. Mozzarella, shredded
- 1 tsp. olive oil
- 8 eggs, beaten
- 1 tsp. ground paprika

Servings: 8
Cooking Time: 5 Hours

Directions:

1. Brush the Slow Cooker bowl with olive oil.
2. In the mixing bowl mix oatmeal, eggs, and ground paprika.
3. Pour the mixture in the Slow Cooker.
4. Add all remaining ingredients, gently stir the mixture.
5. Close the lid and cook the quiche for 5 hours on High.

Quinoa Cauliflower Medley

Ingredients:

- 8 oz. potato, peeled and cubed
- 7 oz. cauliflower, cut in florets
- 1 C. onion, chopped
- 7 oz. chickpea, canned
- 1 C. tomatoes, chopped
- 13 oz. almond milk
- 3 C. chicken stock
- 8 tbsp quinoa
- 1/3 tbsp miso
- 1 tsp minced garlic
- 2 tsp curry paste

Servings: 7

Cooking Time: 9 Hrs

Directions:

1. Spread the chopped potatoes, tomatoes, and onion in the Slow Cooker.
2. Whisk curry paste with chicken stock and miso in a separate bowl.
3. Pour this mixture over the layer of the veggies.
4. Now top this mixture with chickpeas, cauliflower florets, quinoa, garlic, and almond milk.
5. Put the cooker's lid on and set the cooking time to 9 hours on Low settings.
6. Serve.

Eggs And Sweet Potato Mix

Ingredients:

- ½ red onion, chopped
- ½ green bell pepper, chopped
- 2 sweet potatoes, peeled and grated
- ½ red bell pepper, chopped
- 1 garlic clove, minced
- ½ tsp. olive oil
- 4 eggs, whisked
- 1 tbsp. chives, chopped
- A pinch of red pepper, crushed
- A pinch of salt and black pepper

Servings: 2

Cooking Time: 6 Hours

Directions:

1. In a bowl, mix the eggs with the onion, bell peppers and the other ingredients except the oil and whisk well.
2. Grease your Slow Cooker with the oil, add the eggs and potato mix, spread, put the lid on and cook on Low for 6 hours.
3. Divide everything between plates and serve.

Nutmeg Banana Oatmeal

Ingredients:

- Cooking spray
- 2 bananas, sliced
- 1 C. steel-cut oats
- 28 oz. canned coconut milk
- ½ C. of water
- 1 tbsp butter
- 2 tbsp brown sugar
- ¼ tsp nutmeg, ground
- ½ tsp cinnamon powder
- ½ tsp vanilla extract
- 1 tbsp flaxseed, ground

Servings: 6

Cooking Time: 7 Hrs

Directions:

1. Coat the base of your Slow Cooker with cooking spray.
2. Spread oats, banana slices, water, coconut milk, sugar, butter, cinnamon, flaxseed, and vanilla in this cooker.
3. Put the cooker's lid on and set the cooking time to 7 hours on Low settings.
4. Serve fresh.
5. Enjoy.

Thyme Hash Browns

Ingredients:

- Cooking spray
- 10 oz. hash browns
- 2 eggs, whisked
- ¼ C. heavy cream
- ¼ tsp. thyme, dried
- ¼ tsp. garlic powder
- A pinch of salt and black pepper
- ½ C. mozzarella, shredded
- 1 tbsp. chives, chopped
- 1 tbsp. parsley, chopped

Servings: 2
Cooking Time: 4 Hours

Directions:

1. Grease your Slow Cooker with cooking spray, spread the hash browns on the bottom, add the eggs, cream and the other ingredients except the cheese and toss.
2. Sprinkle the cheese on top, put the lid on and cook on High for 4 hours.
3. Divide the mix between plates and serve for breakfast.

Cranberry Oatmeal

Ingredients:

- 1 C. dried cranberries
- 1 C. steel cut oats
- 1 C. dates, chopped
- 4 C. water
- 2 tbsp. honey
- ½ C. half and half

Servings: 4
Cooking Time: 8 Hours 15 Mins.

Directions:

1. Grease a Slow Cooker and add all the ingredients except the half and half and honey.
2. Cover and cook on LOW for about 8 hours.
3. Stir in honey and half and half and dish out to serve.

LUNCH & DINNER RECIPES

Turmeric Lentils Stew

Ingredients:

- 2 C. veggie stock
- ½ C. canned red lentils, drained
- 1 carrot, sliced
- 1 eggplant, cubed
- ½ C. tomatoes, chopped
- 1 red onion, chopped
- 1 garlic clove, minced
- 1 tsp. turmeric powder
- ¼ tbsp. ginger, grated
- ½ tsp. mustard seeds
- ¼ tsp. sweet paprika
- ½ C. tomato paste
- 1 tbsp. dill, chopped
- Salt and black pepper to the taste

Servings: 2

Cooking Time: 5 Hours

Directions:

1. In your Slow Cooker, combine the lentils with the stock, tomatoes, eggplant and the other ingredients, toss, put the lid on, cook on High for 5 hours, divide into bowls and serve.

Mushroom Stroganoff

Ingredients:

- 1 1/2 lb. mushrooms, sliced
- 2 tbsp. all-purpose flour
- 1 onion, chopped
- 4 garlic cloves, chopped
- 2 tbsp. olive oil
- 1/2 tsp. smoked paprika
- 1 C. half and half
- 1/2 C. vegetable stock
- Salt and pepper to taste

Servings: 6

Cooking Time: 6 1/4 Hours

Directions:

1. Heat the oil in a skillet. Add the onion and garlic and cook for 2 minutes then transfer in your Slow Cooker.
2. Sprinkle the mushrooms with flour and coat them well. Place in your Slow Cooker.
3. Add the remaining ingredients and season with salt and pepper.
4. Cook on low settings for 6 hours.
5. Serve the stroganoff warm.

Cacciatore Chicken

Ingredients:

- 2 lb. chicken drumsticks
- 2 tbsp. canola oil
- 2 celery stalks, sliced
- 2 C. sliced mushrooms
- 2 carrots, sliced
- 1 large onion, sliced
- 2 garlic cloves, minced
- 1 red bell pepper, cored and sliced
- 1 yellow bell pepper, cored and sliced
- 1/4 C. dry white wine
- 2 tbsp. tomato paste
- 1 C. chicken stock
- 1 tbsp. cornstarch
- 1/2 tsp. dried oregano
- 1 tsp. dried basil
- 1 bay leaf
- Salt and pepper to taste

Servings: 8
Cooking Time: 7 1/4 Hours

Directions:

1. Heat the canola oil in a skillet or frying pan. Add the chicken and cook on all sides until golden.
2. Transfer the chicken in your Slow Cooker and add the remaining ingredients.
3. Season with salt and pepper and cook on low settings for 7 hours.
4. Serve the chicken warm and fresh.

Chicken And Eggplant Stew

Ingredients:

- 1 C. tomato paste
- ½ C. chicken stock
- 1 lb. chicken breast, skinless, boneless and cubed
- 2 eggplants, cubed
- 1 small red onion, chopped
- 1 red bell pepper, chopped
- ½ tsp. rosemary, dried
- ½ tbsp. smoked paprika
- 1 tsp. cumin, ground
- Cooking spray
- Salt and black pepper to the taste
- Juice of ½ lemon
- ½ tbsp. parsley, chopped

Servings: 2
Cooking Time: 8 Hours

Directions:

1. In your Slow Cooker, mix the chicken with the stock, tomato paste and the other ingredients, toss, put the lid on and cook on Low for 8 hours.
2. Divide into bowls and serve for lunch.

Beef Roast Au Jus

Ingredients:

- 4 lb. rump roast
- 1 tbsp. ground black pepper
- 1 tbsp. smoked paprika
- 1 tsp. chili powder
- 1 tsp. garlic powder
- 1 tsp. mustard seeds
- 1 C. water
- Salt and pepper to taste

Servings: 8
Cooking Time: 10 1/4 Hours

Directions:

1. Mix the black pepper, paprika, chili powder, garlic powder, mustard seeds, salt and pepper in a bowl.
2. Spread this mixture over the beef and rub it well into the meat.
3. Place the beef on your Slow Cooker and add the water.
4. Cover with its lid and cook on low settings for 10 hours.
5. Serve the beef roast sliced and warm.

Slow Cooker Steamed Rice

Ingredients:

- 2 C. white rice
- 4 C. water
- 1 bay leaf
- Salt and pepper to taste

Servings: 8

Cooking Time: 4 Hours

Directions:

1. Combine all the ingredients in your Slow Cooker.
2. Add salt and pepper as needed and cook on low settings for 4 hours. If possible, stir once during the cooking process.
3. Serve the rice warm or chilled, as a side dish to your favorite veggie main dish.

Chunky Beef Pasta Sauce

Ingredients:

- 2 lb. beef sirloin, cut into thin strips
- 1 carrot, diced
- 1 celery stalk, diced
- 2 garlic cloves, chopped
- 1 can (28 oz.) diced tomatoes
- 2 C. sliced mushrooms
- 1/4 C. red wine
- 1 C. tomato sauce
- 1 bay leaf
- Salt and pepper to taste

Servings: 8

Cooking Time: 6 1/2 Hours

Directions:

1. Combine the beef sirloin, carrot, celery, garlic, tomatoes, mushrooms, red wine, tomato sauce and bay leaf in your Slow Cooker.
2. Add enough salt and pepper and cover with its lid.
3. Cook on low settings for 6 hours.
4. Serve the sauce right away with cooked pasta or freeze it into individual portions to serve later.

Garden Beef Stew

Ingredients:

- 3 lb. beef roast, cubed
- 2 tbsp. canola oil
- 2 red bell peppers, cored and sliced
- 2 yellow bell peppers, cored and sliced
- 1 C. tomato sauce
- 2 C. cherry tomatoes
- 2 bay leaves
- 1 thyme sprig
- 1 pinch cayenne pepper
- Salt to taste

Servings: 8
Cooking Time: 7 1/4 Hours

Directions:

1. Heat the canola oil in a large frying pan and add the beef. Cook for a few minutes on all sides until golden then transfer in your Slow Cooker.
2. Add the remaining ingredients and season with salt as needed.
3. Cover the pot with its lid and cook on low settings for 7 hours.
4. Serve the stew warm.

Salsa Chicken (1)

Ingredients:

- 7 oz. mild salsa
- 1 lb. chicken breast, skinless, boneless and cubed
- 1 small yellow onion, chopped
- ½ tsp. coriander, ground
- ½ tsp. rosemary, dried
- 1 green bell pepper, chopped
- Cooking spray
- 1 tbsp. cilantro, chopped
- 1 red bell pepper, chopped
- 1 tbsp. chili powder

Servings: 2
Cooking Time: 8 Hours

Directions:

1. Grease the Slow Cooker with the cooking spray and mix the chicken with the salsa, onion and the other ingredients inside.
2. Put the lid on, cook on Low for 8 hours, divide into bowls and serve for lunch.

DESSERT
RECIPES

Vanilla Cookies

Ingredients:

- 2 eggs
- ¼ C. vegetable oil
- 1 C. sugar
- ½ tsp. vanilla extract
- 1 tsp. baking powder
- 1 and ½ C. almond meal
- ½ C. almonds, chopped

Servings: 12

Cooking Time: 2 Hours And 30 Mins.

Directions:

1. In a bowl, mix oil with sugar, vanilla extract and eggs and whisk.
2. Add baking powder, almond meal and almonds and stir well.
3. Line your Slow Cooker with parchment paper, spread cookie mix on the bottom of the Slow Cooker, cover and cook on Low for 2 hours and 30 minutes.
4. Leave cookie sheet to cool down, cut into medium pieces and serve.

Creamy Berries Mix

Ingredients:

- ½ tsp. nutmeg, ground
- ½ tsp. vanilla extract
- ½ C. blackberries
- ½ C. blueberries
- ¼ C. whipping cream
- 1 tbsp. sugar
- 2 tbsp. walnuts, chopped

Servings: 2

Cooking Time: 1 Hour

Directions:

1. In your Slow Cooker, combine the berries with the cream and the other ingredients, toss gently, put the lid on, cook on High for 1 hour, divide into bowls, and serve.

Cottage Cheese Corners

Ingredients:

- 2 tbsp. cottage cheese
- 1 tsp. sugar
- 1 tsp. vanilla extract
- 1 egg, beaten
- 3 oz puff pastry
- Cooking spray

Servings: 3
Cooking Time: 3 Hours

Directions:

1. Mix cottage cheese with sugar, vanilla extract, and ½ of the beaten egg.
2. Stir the mixture until smooth.
3. Then roll up the puff pastry and cut it in the shape of squares.
4. Spread every dough square with a cottage cheese mixture.
5. Then wrap them in the shape of corners.
6. Spray the Slow Cooker bowl with cooking spray.
7. Put the corners inside and close the lid.
8. Cook them on High for 3 hours.

Vanilla And Cocoa Pudding

Ingredients:

- 1 C. of coconut milk
- 1 tbsp. cornflour
- 1 tsp. vanilla extract
- 1 tbsp. brown sugar
- 1 tbsp. butter
- 2 tbsp. cocoa powder

Servings: 2

Cooking Time: 7 Hours

Directions:

1. Mix coconut milk with cocoa powder, brown sugar, vanilla extract, and cornflour.
2. Whisk the mixture until smooth and transfer in the Slow Cooker.
3. Add butter and close the lid.
4. Cook the pudding on Low for 7 hours.
5. Then transfer it in the serving bowls and cool to the room temperature.

Cherry Jam

Ingredients:

- 2 C. cherries, pitted
- ½ C. of sugar
- 1 tbsp. agar
- 3 tbsp. water

Servings: 4

Cooking Time: 3 Hours

Directions:

1. Mix sugar with cherries and put in the Slow Cooker.
2. Then mix water and agar and pour the liquid in the Slow Cooker too.
3. Stir well and close the lid.
4. Cook the jam on high for 3 hours.
5. Then transfer the jam in the glass cans and store it in the fridge for up to 2 months.

Pear And Apple Butter

Ingredients:

- 6 large red apples, peeled, cored and sliced
- 4 ripe pears, peeled, cored and sliced
- 1 1/2 C. fresh apple juice
- 1 C. white sugar
- 1 C. light brown sugar
- 1 cinnamon stick
- 4 cardamom pods, crushed

Servings: 6

Cooking Time: 6 1/2 Hours

Directions:

1. Combine all the ingredients in your Slow Cooker.
2. Cover the pot and cook on low settings for 6 hours.
3. When done, pour the mixture into glass jars and seal them with a lid.
4. Allow to cool before serving.

Rhubarb Stew

Ingredients:

- ½ lb. rhubarb, roughly sliced
- 2 tbsp. sugar
- ½ tsp. vanilla extract
- ½ tsp. lemon extract
- 1 tbsp. lemon juice
- ¼ C. water

Servings: 2

Cooking Time: 2 Hours

Directions:

1. In your Slow Cooker, mix the rhubarb with the sugar, vanilla and the other ingredients, toss, put the lid on and cook on Low for 2 hours.
2. Divide the mix into bowls and serve cold.

Sweet Tabbouleh

Ingredients:

- 1 C. bulgur
- 2 C. of water
- 1 orange, peeled, chopped
- 3 dates, chopped
- 1 tbsp. coconut shred
- 2 tbsp. of liquid honey
- 1 tbsp. raisins

Servings: 6
Cooking Time: 2.5 Hours

Directions:

1. Mix bulgur and water and transfer in the Slow Cooker.
2. Cook it on High for 5 hours.
3. Then cool the bulgur and transfer in the mixing bowl.
4. Add all remaining ingredients and carefully mix.

Pumpkin Balls

Ingredients:

- ½ C. pumpkin puree
- ¼ C. of sugar
- 4 tbsp. flour
- 1 tsp. olive oil

Servings: 4
Cooking Time: 2 Hours

Directions:

1. Mix pumpkin puree with sugar.
2. Then add flour and knead the soft dough.
3. Make the balls from the pumpkin mixture.
4. After this, brush the Slow Cooker bottom with olive oil.
5. Put the pumpkin balls in the Slow Cooker in one layer and close the lid.
6. Cook the pumpkin balls on High for 2 hours.

BEEF, PORK & LAMB RECIPES

Herbed Pork Tenderloin

Ingredients:

- 2 pork tenderloins, skin removed
- ½ C. extra virgin olive oil
- ½ C. apple cider vinegar
- ½ C. cilantro, chopped
- 3 green onions, chopped
- 2 jalapeno peppers, chopped
- 2 tbsp. ginger, grated
- 1 tsp. salt
- ½ tsp. ground black pepper
- ½ tsp. all spice
- 1/8 tsp. ground cloves

Servings: 6
Cooking Time: 12 Hours

Directions:

1. Mix all ingredients in a bowl and allow meat to marinate in the fridge for at least 2 hours.
2. Line aluminum foil at the base of the Slow Cooker.
3. Place the meat.
4. Close the lid and cook on high for 10 hours or on low for 12 hours.

Cajun Pork Loin

Ingredients:

- 12 oz pork loin
- 1 tbsp. Cajun seasonings
- 2 tbsp. sunflower oil
- ½ C. of water
- 3 garlic cloves, sliced

Servings: 3

Cooking Time: 7 Hours

Directions:

1. Rub the pork loin with Cajun seasonings and sprinkle with sunflower oil.
2. Transfer the meat in the Slow Cooker.
3. Add water and garlic cloves.
4. Close the lid and cook the meat on low for 7 hours.

Maple Syrup Sliced Belly

Ingredients:

- 8 oz pork belly, sliced
- ¼ C. maple syrup
- 3 tbsp. butter, melted
- 1 tsp. ground coriander
- ½ tsp. garlic powder
- ¼ tsp. salt
- 1 tbsp. sesame oil

Servings: 4

Cooking Time: 8 Hours

Directions:

1. Mix butter with maple syrup, ground coriander, garlic powder, and salt.
2. After this, add sesame oil and whisk the mixture until smooth.
3. Mix the sliced pork belly with maple syrup mixture and put it in the Slow Cooker.
4. Add all remaining maple syrup liquid and close the lid.
5. Cook the meal on Low for 8 hours. Add water in pork belly if needed.

Beef Chuck Roast

Ingredients:

- 4 lb. beef chuck roast
- 1 C. veggie stock
- 1 tbsp. coconut oil
- 1 bay leaf
- 10 thyme springs
- 4 garlic cloves, minced
- 1 carrot, roughly chopped
- 1 yellow onion, roughly chopped
- 2 celery ribs, roughly chopped
- 1 cauliflower head, florets separated
- Salt and black pepper to the taste

Servings: 6

Cooking Time: 8 Hours And 30 Mins.

Directions:

1. Season beef with salt and some black pepper.
2. Heat up a pan with the oil over medium-high heat, add beef roast, brown for 5 minutes on each side, transfer to your Slow Cooker, add thyme springs, stock, bay leaf, garlic, celery, onion and carrot, cover and cook on Low for 8 hours.
3. Add cauliflower, cover Slow Cooker again, cook on High for 20 minutes more, divide everything between plates and serve.

Maple Beef

Ingredients:

- 1 lb. beef roast, sliced
- 1 tbsp. maple syrup
- 2 tbsp. balsamic vinegar
- 2 tsp. olive oil
- ½ tsp. Italian seasoning
- A pinch of salt and black pepper
- 1 tbsp. coriander, chopped
- ½ C. beef stock

Servings: 2
Cooking Time: 7 Hours

Directions:

1. In your Slow Cooker, mix the roast with the maple syrup, vinegar and the other ingredients, toss, put the lid on and cook on Low for 7 hours.
2. Divide the mix between plates and serve.

Paprika Lamb

Ingredients:

- 1 lb. lamb chops
- 1 tbsp. sweet paprika
- ½ C. beef stock
- 2 tbsp. avocado oil
- 2 scallions, chopped
- A pinch of salt and black pepper

Servings: 2
Cooking Time: 4 Hours

Directions:

1. In your Slow Cooker, mix the lamb chops with the paprika, stock and the other ingredients, toss, put the lid on and cook on High for 4 hours.
2. Divide the mix between plates and serve with a side salad.

Bacon Swiss Pork Chops

Ingredients:

- 8 pork chops, bone in
- 2 tbsp. olive oil
- 4 cloves of garlic
- 12 bacon strips, cut in half
- 1 C. Swiss cheese, shredded

Servings: 8
Cooking Time: 10 Hours

Directions:

1. Season the pork chops with salt and pepper to taste
2. In a skillet, heat the olive oil over medium flame and sauté the garlic until fragrant and slightly golden.
3. Transfer to the Slow Cooker.
4. Wrap the bacon strips around the pork chops.
5. Place in the Slow Cooker and sprinkle with shredded Swiss cheese.
6. Close the lid and cook on low for 10 hours or on high for 8 hours.

Pork Loin And Cauliflower Rice

Ingredients:

- 3 bacon slices, cooked and chopped
- 3 carrots, chopped
- 2 lb. pork loin roast
- 1 rhubarb stalk, chopped
- 2 bay leaves
- ¼ C. red wine vinegar
- 4 garlic cloves, minced
- Salt and black pepper to the taste
- ¼ C. olive oil
- 1 tbsp. garlic powder
- 1 tbsp. Italian seasoning
- 24 oz. cauliflower rice
- 1 tsp. turmeric powder
- 1 C. beef stock

Servings: 6
Cooking Time: 8 Hours

Directions:

1. In your Slow Cooker, mix bacon with carrots, pork, rhubarb, bay leaves, vinegar, salt, pepper, oil, garlic powder, Italian seasoning, stock and turmeric, toss, cover and cook on Low for 7 hours.
2. Add cauliflower rice, cover, cook on Low for 1 more hour, divide between plates and serve.

Stuffed Pork

Ingredients:

- Zest of 2 limes
- Juice of 1 orange
- Zest of 1 orange
- Juice of 2 limes
- 4 tsp. garlic, minced
- ¾ C. olive oil
- 1 C. cilantro, chopped
- 1 C. mint, chopped
- 1 tsp. oregano, dried
- Salt and black pepper to the taste
- 2 tsp. cumin, ground
- 4 pork loin steaks
- 2 pickles, chopped
- 4 ham slices
- 6 Swiss cheese slices
- 2 tbsp. mustard

Servings: 4
Cooking Time: 8 Hours

Directions:

1. In your food processor, mix lime zest and juice with orange zest and juice, garlic, oil, cilantro, mint, oregano, cumin, salt and pepper and blend well.
2. Season steaks with salt and pepper, place them in a bowl, add marinade you've made, toss to coat and leave aside for a couple of hours.
3. Place steaks on a working surface, divide pickles, cheese, mustard and ham on them, roll, secure with toothpicks, put them in your Slow Cooker, cover and cook on Low for 7 hours.
4. Divide between plates and serve.

POULTRY RECIPES

Creamy Bacon Chicken

Ingredients:

- 5 oz. bacon, cooked
- 8 oz. chicken breast
- 1 garlic clove, peeled and chopped
- ½ carrot, peeled and chopped
- 1 C. heavy cream
- 1 egg, beaten
- 1 tbsp paprika
- 1 tsp curry
- 3 tbsp chives, chopped
- 3 oz. scallions, chopped

Servings: 4

Cooking Time: 12 Hours

Directions:

1. Carve a cut in the chicken breasts from sideways.
2. Stuff the chicken with garlic clove and carrot.
3. Place the stuffed chicken in the Slow Cooker.
4. Mix egg with cream, paprika, curry, scallions, and paprika in a bowl.
5. Pour this curry mixture over the chicken and top it with chives and bacon.
6. Add the remaining ingredients to the cooker.
7. Put the cooker's lid on and set the cooking time to 12 hours on Low settings.
8. Shred the slow-cooked chicken and return to the cooker.
9. Mix well and serve.

Sweet And Hot Chicken Wings

Ingredients:

- 12 chicken wings, cut into 24 pieces
- 1 lb. celery, cut into thin matchsticks
- ¼ C. honey
- 4 tbsp. hot sauce
- Salt to the taste
- ¼ C. tomato puree
- 1 C. yogurt
- 1 tbsp. parsley, chopped

Servings: 6

Cooking Time: 4 Hours

Directions:

1. In your Slow Cooker, mix chicken with celery, honey, hot sauce, salt, tomato puree and parsley, stir, cover and cook on High for 3 hours and 30 minutes.
2. Add yogurt, toss, cover, cook on High for 30 minutes more, divide between plates and serve

Bacon Chicken Wings

Ingredients:

- 4 chicken wings, boneless
- 4 bacon slices
- 1 tbsp. maple syrup
- ½ tsp. ground black pepper
- ½ C. of water

Servings: 4

Cooking Time: 3 Hours

Directions:

1. Sprinkle the chicken wings with ground black pepper and maple syrup.
2. Then wrap every chicken wing in the bacon and place it in the Slow Cooker.
3. Add water and close the lid.
4. Cook the chicken wings in High for 3 hours.

Pineapple Chicken

Ingredients:

- 12 oz chicken fillet
- 1 C. pineapple, canned, chopped
- ½ C. Cheddar cheese, shredded
- 1 tbsp. butter, softened
- 1 tsp. ground black pepper
- ¼ C. of water

Servings: 4

Cooking Time: 8 Hours

Directions:

1. Grease the Slow Cooker bowl bottom with softened butter.
2. Then cut the chicken fillet into servings and put in the Slow Cooker in one layer.
3. After this, top the chicken with ground black pepper, water, pineapple, and Cheddar cheese.
4. Close the lid and cook the meal on Low for 8 hours.

Simple Buttered Rosemary Chicken Breasts

Ingredients:

- 5 tbsp. butter
- 4 boneless chicken breasts
- Salt and pepper to taste
- 1 tbsp. parsley
- 1 tsp. rosemary

Servings: 4

Cooking Time: 6 Hours

Directions:

1. Melt the butter in the skillet.
2. Season chicken with salt and pepper to taste. Brown all sides of the chicken for 3 minutes.
3. Transfer into the Slow Cooker and sprinkle with parsley and rosemary.
4. Cook on low for 6 hours or on high for 5 hours.

Chicken And Dumplings

Ingredients:

- 1 yellow onion, chopped
- 1 and ½ lb. chicken breast, skinless and boneless
- Salt and black pepper to the taste
- 1 tsp. oregano, dried
- 2 C. cream of chicken soup
- 2 C. chicken stock
- 4 thyme springs, chopped
- 1 bay leaf
- 2 celery stalks, chopped
- 2 carrots, chopped
- 1 C. peas
- 3 garlic cloves, minced
- ½ C. parmesan, grated
- 1 biscuit dough tube, cut into small pieces
- 1 tbsp. parsley, chopped

Servings: 4

Cooking Time: 4 Hours

Directions:

1. In your Slow Cooker, mix onion with chicken, oregano, salt, pepper, cream of chicken soup, chicken stock, bay leaf and thyme, stir, cover and cook on High for 3 hours.
2. Discard bay leaf, add celery, carrots, peas, garlic and biscuit pieces, stir, cover and cook on High for 1 hour.
3. Add parmesan and parsley, divide into bowls and serve.

Slow Cooker Chicken Thighs

Ingredients:

- 5 lb. chicken thighs
- Salt and black pepper to the taste
- ½ C. white vinegar
- 1 tsp. black peppercorns
- 4 garlic cloves, minced
- 3 bay leaves
- ½ C. soy sauce

Servings: 6
Cooking Time: 4 Hours

Directions:

1. In your Slow Cooker mix chicken, vinegar, soy sauce, salt, pepper, garlic, peppercorns and bay leaves, stir, cover and cook on High for 4 hours.
2. Discard bay leaves, stir, divide chicken mix between plates and serve.

Chicken And Tomatillos

Ingredients:

- 1 lb. chicken thighs, skinless and boneless
- 2 tbsp. olive oil
- 1 yellow onion, chopped
- 1 garlic clove, minced
- 4 oz. canned green chilies, chopped
- A handful cilantro, chopped
- Salt and black pepper to the taste
- 15 oz. canned tomatillos, chopped
- 5 oz. canned garbanzo beans, drained
- 15 oz. rice, cooked
- 5 oz. tomatoes, chopped
- 15 oz. cheddar cheese, grated
- 4 oz. black olives, pitted and chopped

Servings: 6
Cooking Time: 4 Hours

Directions:

1. In your Slow Cooker, mix oil with onions, garlic, chicken, chilies, salt, pepper, cilantro and tomatillos, stir, cover the Slow Cooker and cook on High for 3 hours
2. Take chicken out of the Slow Cooker, shred, return to Slow Cooker, add rice, beans, cheese, tomatoes and olives, cover and cook on High for 1 more hour.
3. Divide between plates and serve.

FISH & SEAFOOD
RECIPES

Seafood Bean Chili

Ingredients:

- 1 lb. salmon, diced
- 7 oz shrimps, peeled
- 1 tbsp salt
- 1 C. tomatoes, canned
- 1 tsp ground white pepper
- 1 tbsp tomato sauce
- 2 onions, chopped
- 1 C. carrot, chopped
- 1 can red beans
- ½ C. tomato juice
- 1 C. fish stock
- 1 tsp cayenne pepper
- 1 C. bell pepper, chopped
- 1 tbsp olive oil
- 1 tsp coriander
- 1 C. of water
- 6 oz Parmesan, shredded
- 1 garlic clove, sliced

Servings: 8
Cooking Time: 3.5 Hrs.

Directions:

1. Add tomatoes, white pepper, tomato sauce, red beans, carrots, tomato juice, bell pepper, fish stock, cayenne pepper, garlic, water and coriander to the insert of Slow Cooker.
2. Put the cooker's lid on and set the cooking time to 3 hours on High settings.
3. Add olive oil and seafood to a suitable pan, then sauté for 3 minutes.
4. Transfer the sautéed seafood to the Slow Cooker.
5. Put the cooker's lid on and set the cooking time to 30 minutes on High settings.
6. Serve warm.

Mushroom And Shrimp Curry

Ingredients:

- 1 lb. shrimp, peeled and deveined
- 1 C. bouillon
- 4 lemon slices
- Salt and black pepper to the taste
- ½ tsp. curry powder
- ¼ C. mushrooms, sliced
- ¼ C. yellow onion, chopped
- 1 tbsp. olive oil
- ½ C. raisins
- 3 tbsp. flour
- 1 C. milk

Servings: 4

Cooking Time: 2 Hours And 30 Mins.

Directions:

1. In your Slow Cooker, mix bouillon with lemon, salt, pepper, curry powder, mushrooms, onion, flour and milk, whisk well, cover and cook on High for 2 hours.
2. Add shrimp and raisins, cover and cook on High for 30 minutes more.
3. Divide curry into bowls and serve.

Calamari Curry

Ingredients:

- 1 lb. calamari rings
- ½ tbsp. yellow curry paste
- 1 C. coconut milk
- ½ tsp. turmeric powder
- ½ C. chicken stock
- 2 garlic cloves, minced
- ½ tbsp. coriander, chopped
- A pinch of salt and black pepper
- 2 tbsp. lemon juice

Servings: 2

Cooking Time: 3 Hours

Directions:

1. In your Slow Cooker, mix the rings with the curry paste, coconut milk and the other ingredients, toss, put the lid on and cook on High for 3 hours.
2. Divide the curry into bowls and serve.

Mustard Garlic Shrimps

Ingredients:

- 1 tsp. olive oil
- 3 tbsp. garlic, minced
- 1-lb. shrimp, shelled and deveined
- 1 tsp. Dijon mustards
- Salt and pepper to taste
- Parsley for garnish

Servings: 4

Cooking Time: 2 Hours And 30 Mins.

Directions:

1. In a skillet, heat the olive oil and sauté the garlic until fragrant and slightly browned.
2. Transfer to the Slow Cooker and place the shrimps and Dijon mustard. Stir to combine.
3. Season with salt and pepper to taste.
4. Close the lid and cook on low for 2 hours or high for 30 minutes.
5. Once done, sprinkle with parsley.

Salmon With Saffron Rice

Ingredients:

- 2 wild salmon fillets, boneless
- Salt and black pepper to the taste
- ½ C. jasmine rice
- 1 C. chicken stock
- ¼ C. veggie stock
- 1 tbsp butter
- A pinch of saffron

Servings: 2

Cooking Time: 2 Hrs.

Directions:

1. Add stock, rice, butter, and saffron to the insert of Slow Cooker.
2. Mix well, then add salmon, salt, and black pepper to the cooker.
3. Put the cooker's lid on and set the cooking time to 2 hours on High settings.
4. Serve warm.

Taco Mahi Mahi

Ingredients:

- 2-lb. Mahi Mahi fillets
- 1 tbsp. taco seasonings
- 1 tsp. fish sauce
- 1/3 C. chicken stock
- 1 tbsp. sunflower oil

Servings: 6
Cooking Time: 6 Hours

Directions:

1. Sprinkle the fish fillets with taco seasonings and fish sauce.
2. Pour sunflower oil in the Slow Cooker.
3. Add fish and chicken stock.
4. Close the lid and cook the fish on Low for 6 hours.

Fish And Mac Casserole

Ingredients:

- ½ C. Cheddar cheese, shredded
- 2 cod fillets, chopped
- 6 oz macaroni, cooked
- 1 tsp. coconut oil
- 1 tsp. white pepper
- 1/2 C. cream cheese

Servings: 6
Cooking Time: 2 Hours

Directions:

1. Put cream cheese in the Slow Cooker.
2. Add coconut oil, white pepper, and chopped cod.
3. Cook the fish on high for 1.5 hours.
4. Then add cooked macaroni and Cheddar cheese.
5. Carefully mix the mixture and cook it on High for 30 minutes.

Slow Cooker Seafood Jambalaya

Ingredients:

- 1 onion, chopped
- 2 tbsp. olive oil
- 2 ribs of celery, sliced
- 1 green bell pepper, seeded and chopped
- 1 C. tomatoes, crushed
- 1 C. chicken broth
- 2 tsp. dried oregano
- 2 tsp. dried parsley
- 2 tsp. organic Cajun seasoning
- 1 tsp. cayenne pepper
- 1-lb. shrimps, shelled and deveined
- ½ lb. squid, cleaned
- 2 C. grated cauliflower

Servings: 7

Cooking Time: 3 Hours

Directions:

1. Place all ingredients in the Slow Cooker.
2. Give a good stir.
3. Close the lid and cook on high for 2 hours or on low for 3 hours.

SOUPS & STEWS RECIPES

Mexican Style Stew

Ingredients:

- 1 C. corn kernels
- 1 C. green peas
- ¼ C. white rice
- 4 C. chicken stock
- 1 tsp. taco seasoning
- 1 tsp. dried cilantro
- 1 tbsp. butter

Servings: 6

Cooking Time: 6 Hours

Directions:

1. Put butter and wild rice in the Slow Cooker.
2. Then add corn kernels, green peas, chicken stock, taco seasoning, and dried cilantro.
3. Close the lid and cook the stew on Low for 6 hours.

Ginger Fish Stew

Ingredients:

- 1 oz fresh ginger, peeled, chopped
- 1 C. baby carrot
- 1-lb. salmon fillet, chopped
- 1 tsp. fish sauce
- ½ tsp. ground nutmeg
- ½ C. green peas
- 3 C. of water

Servings: 5

Cooking Time: 6 Hours

Directions:

1. Put all ingredients in the Slow Cooker bowl.
2. Gently stir the stew ingredients and close the lid.
3. Cook the stew on low for 6 hours.

Pumpkin Hearty Soup

Ingredients:

- 2 tbsp. olive oil
- 2 shallots, chopped
- 2 garlic cloves, chopped
- 1 red chili, seeded and chopped
- 1/4 tsp. grated ginger
- 2 tbsp. tomato paste
- 1 can diced tomatoes
- 1 can (15 oz.) black beans, drained
- 2 C. pumpkin cubes
- 2 C. water
- 3 C. vegetable stock
- 1 bay leaf
- Salt and pepper to taste
- 1/2 cinnamon stick
- 1/4 tsp. cumin powder

Servings: 10
Cooking Time: 6 1/4 Hours

Directions:

1. Heat the oil in a skillet or saucepan and add the shallots, garlic, red chili and ginger. Cook for 3-4 minutes then transfer in your Slow Cooker.
2. Add the tomato paste, tomatoes, black beans and pumpkin, as well as the water, stock, bay leaf, cinnamon and cumin.
3. Adjust the taste with salt and cook on low settings for 6 hours.
4. Serve the soup warm and fresh.

Spicy White Chicken Soup

Ingredients:

- 2 chicken breasts, cubed
- 2 tbsp. olive oil
- 1 large onion, chopped
- 2 garlic cloves, chopped
- 2 C. chicken stock
- 1 parsnip, diced
- 1/2 tsp. cumin seeds
- 1/4 tsp. cayenne pepper
- 1/2 tsp. dried oregano
- 1/2 tsp. dried basil
- 2 cans (15 oz.) white beans, drained
- 5 C. water
- 1 bay leaf
- Salt and pepper to taste

Servings: 8
Cooking Time: 6 1/4 Hours

Directions:

1. Heat the oil in a skillet and add the chicken. Cook on all sides until golden then transfer in your Slow Cooker.
2. Add the onion, garlic, stock, parsnip, cumin seeds, cayenne pepper, oregano, basil, beans, water and bay leaf.
3. Adjust the taste with salt and pepper and cook on low settings for 6 hours.
4. Serve the soup warm and fresh.

Roasted Chicken Stock

Ingredients:

- 1 whole chicken, cut into smaller pieces
- 2 carrots, cut in half
- 1 parsnip
- 1 celery root, peeled and sliced
- 2 onions, halved
- 10 C. water
- 1 bay leaf
- 1 rosemary sprig
- 1 thyme sprig
- Salt and pepper to taste

Servings: 10

Cooking Time: 9 Hours

Directions:

1. Season the chicken with salt and pepper and place it in a baking tray. Roast in the preheated oven at 400F for 40 minutes.
2. Transfer the chicken in your Slow Cooker and add the remaining ingredients.
3. Season with salt and pepper and cook on low settings for 8 hours.
4. Use the stock right away or store in the fridge or freezer.

Moroccan Lentil Soup

Ingredients:

- 1 large sweet onion, chopped
- 2 garlic cloves, chopped
- 2 tbsp. olive oil
- 2 carrots, diced
- 1 parsnip, diced
- 1 C. chopped cauliflower
- 1/2 tsp. cumin powder
- 1/4 tsp. turmeric powder
- 1/2 tsp. ground coriander
- 2 C. water
- 3 C. chicken stock
- 1 C. red lentils
- 2 tbsp. tomato paste
- 2 tbsp. lemon juice
- Salt and pepper to taste

Servings: 6

Cooking Time: 6 1/4 Hours

Directions:

1. Heat the oil in a skillet and stir in the onion, garlic, carrots and parsnip. Cook for 5 minutes then transfer in your Slow Cooker.
2. Stir in the cauliflower, cumin powder, turmeric and coriander, as well as water, stock, lentils and tomato paste.
3. Add the lemon juice, salt and pepper and cook on low settings for 6 hours.
4. Serve the soup warm or chilled.

Sweet Corn Chowder

Ingredients:

- 2 shallots, chopped
- 4 medium size potatoes, peeled and cubed1
- 1 celery stalk, sliced
- 1 can (15 oz.) sweet corn, drained
- 2 C. chicken stock
- 2 C. water
- Salt and pepper to taste

Servings: 8
Cooking Time: 6 1/4 Hours

Directions:

1. Combine the shallot, potatoes, celery, corn, stock and water in a Slow Cooker.
2. Add salt and pepper to taste and cook on low settings for 6 hours.
3. When done, remove a few tbsp. of corn from the pot then puree the remaining soup in the pot.
4. Pour the soup into serving bowls and top with the reserved corn.
5. Serve warm.

Ham And White Bean Soup

Ingredients:

- 2 tbsp. olive oil
- 1 sweet onion, chopped
- 1 garlic clove, chopped
- 1 yellow bell pepper, cored and diced
- 1 celery stalk, diced
- 1 C. diced ham
- 2 cans (15 oz.) white beans, drained
- 2 C. chicken stock
- 3 C. water
- Salt and pepper to taste
- 2 tbsp. chopped parsley

Servings: 8
Cooking Time: 6 1/4 Hours

Directions:

1. Heat the oil in a skillet and stir in the onion, garlic, celery and bell pepper. Sauté for 5 minutes until softened and transfer in your Slow Cooker.
2. Add the ham, white beans, stock and water and season with salt and pepper.
3. Cook on low settings for 6 hours.
4. To serve, pour the soup into bowls and top with parsley. The soup can be served both warm and chilled.

APPETIZERS
RECIPES

Spicy Monterey Jack Fondue

Ingredients:

- 1 garlic clove
- 1 C. white wine
- 2 C. grated Monterey Jack cheese
- 1/2 C. grated Parmesan
- 1 red chili, seeded and chopped
- 1 tbsp. cornstarch
- 1/2 C. milk
- 1 pinch nutmeg
- 1 pinch salt
- 1 pinch ground black pepper

Servings: 6

Cooking Time: 4 1/4 Hours

Directions:

1. Rub the inside of your Crock Pot's pot with a garlic clove just to infuse it with aroma.
2. Add the white wine into the pot and stir in the cheeses, red chili, cornstarch and milk.
3. Season with nutmeg, salt and black pepper and cook on low heat for 4 hours.
4. The fondue is best served warm with bread sticks or vegetables.

Rosemary Potatoes

Ingredients:

- 4 lb. small new potatoes
- 1 rosemary sprig, chopped
- 1 shallot, sliced
- 2 garlic cloves, chopped
- 1 tsp. smoked paprika
- 1 tsp. salt
- 1/4 tsp. ground black pepper
- 1/4 C. chicken stock

Servings: 8
Cooking Time: 2 1/4 Hours

Directions:

1. Combine all the ingredients in your Slow Cooker.
2. Cover with its lid and cook on high settings for 2 hours.
3. Serve the potatoes warm or chilled.

Asian Marinated Mushrooms

Ingredients:

- 2 lb. mushrooms
- 1 C. soy sauce
- 1 C. water
- 1/2 C. brown sugar
- 1/4 C. rice vinegar
- 1/2 tsp. chili powder

Servings: 8
Cooking Time: 8 1/4 Hours

Directions:

1. Combine all the ingredients in your Slow Cooker.
2. Cover the Slow Cooker and cook on low settings for 8 hours.
3. Allow to cool in the pot before serving.

Sausage And Pepper Appetizer

Ingredients:

- 6 fresh pork sausages, skins removed
- 2 tbsp. olive oil
- 1 can fire roasted tomatoes
- 4 roasted bell peppers, chopped
- 1 poblano pepper, chopped
- 1 shallot, chopped
- 1 C. grated Provolone cheese
- Salt and pepper to taste

Servings: 8
Cooking Time: 6 1/4 Hours

Directions:

1. Heat the oil in a skillet and stir in the sausage meat. Cook for 5 minutes, stirring often.
2. Transfer the meat in your Slow Cooker and add the remaining ingredients.
3. Season with salt and pepper and cook on low settings for 6 hours.
4. Serve the dish warm or chilled.

Classic Bread In A Slow Cooker

Ingredients:

- 2 tsp. active dry yeast
- 1 tsp. sugar
- 1 C. warm water
- 1/2 C. yogurt
- 1 egg
- 2 tbsp. olive oil
- 3 C. all-purpose flour
- 1/2 tsp. salt

Servings: 8

Cooking Time: 1 1/2 Hours

Directions:

1. Mix the yeast, sugar, warm water, yogurt, egg and olive oil in a bowl.
2. Stir in the flour and salt and mix well. Knead the dough for 5-10 minutes until even and non-sticky.
3. Place the dough in your Slow Cooker and cover with its lid.
4. Cook on high settings for 1 1/4 hours.
5. Serve the bread warm or chilled.

Blue Cheese Chicken Wings

Ingredients:

- 4 lb. chicken wings
- 1/2 C. buffalo sauce
- 1/2 C. spicy tomato sauce
- 1 tbsp. tomato paste
- 2 tbsp. apple cider vinegar
- 1 tbsp. Worcestershire sauce
- 1 C. sour cream
- 2 oz. blue cheese, crumbled
- 1 thyme sprig

Servings: 8

Cooking Time: 7 1/4 Hours

Directions:

1. Combine the buffalo sauce, tomato sauce, vinegar, Worcestershire sauce, sour cream, blue cheese and thyme in a Slow Cooker.
2. Add the chicken wings and toss them until evenly coated.
3. Cook on low settings for 7 hours.
4. Serve the chicken wings preferably warm.

Southwestern Nacho Dip

Ingredients:

- 1 lb. ground pork
- 1 C. apple juice
- 4 garlic cloves, chopped
- 2 C. BBQ sauce
- 2 tbsp. brown sugar
- Salt and pepper to taste
- 1 1/2 C. sweet corn
- 1 can black beans, drained
- 1 C. diced tomatoes
- 2 jalapeno peppers, chopped
- 2 tbsp. chopped cilantro
- 2 C. grated Cheddar
- 1 lime, juiced
- Nachos for serving

Servings: 10
Cooking Time: 6 1/4 Hours

Directions:

1. Heat a skillet over medium flame and add the pork. Cook for a few minutes, stirring often.
2. Transfer the pork in your Slow Cooker and add the apple juice, garlic, BBQ sauce, brown sugar, salt and pepper.
3. Cook on high settings for 2 hours.
4. After 2 hours, add the remaining ingredients and continue cooking for 4 hours on low settings.
5. Serve the dip warm with nachos.

Cheese And Beer Fondue

Ingredients:

- 4 tbsp. butter
- 1 shallot, chopped
- 2 garlic cloves, minced
- 2 tbsp. all-purpose flour
- 2 poblano peppers, chopped
- 1 C. milk
- 1 C. light beer
- 2 C. grated Cheddar
- 1/2 tsp. chili powder

Servings: 10
Cooking Time: 2 1/4 Hours

Directions:

1. Melt the butter in a saucepan and stir in the shallot and garlic. Sauté for 2 minutes then add the flour and cook for 2 additional minutes.
2. Stir in the milk and cook until thickened, about 5 minutes.
3. Pour the mixture in your Slow Cooker and stir in the remaining ingredients.
4. Cook on high settings for 2 hours and serve the fondue warm with biscuits or other salty snacks.

SNACK RECIPES

Wild Rice Pilaf

Servings: 8

Cooking Time: 3 Hours And 10 Mins.

Directions:

1. Place all the ingredients in Slow-Cooker except the seasonings and lemon rind, and give it a good stir. Close the lid and cook on HIGH for 1 ½ hours or on LOW for 3 hours. After done cooking add seasoning to taste. Sprinkle with lemon rind and serve hot.

White Bean Spread

Ingredients:

- ½ C. white beans, dried
- 2 tbsp. cashews, chopped
- 1 tsp. apple cider vinegar
- 1 C. veggie stock
- 1 tbsp. water

Servings: 4

Cooking Time: 7 Hours

Directions:

1. In your Slow Cooker, mix beans with cashews and stock, stir, cover and cook on Low for 6 hours.
2. Drain, transfer to your food processor, add vinegar and water, pulse well, divide into bowls and serve as a spread.

Tamales

Ingredients:

- 8 oz. dried corn husks, soaked for 1 day and drained
- 4 C. water
- 3 lb. pork shoulder, boneless and chopped
- 1 yellow onion, chopped
- 2 garlic cloves, crushed
- 1 tbsp. chipotle chili powder
- 2 tbsp. chili powder
- Salt and black pepper to the taste
- 1 tsp. cumin, ground
- 4 C. masa harina
- ¼ C. corn oil
- ¼ C. shortening
- 1 tsp. baking powder

Servings: 24

Cooking Time: 8 Hours And 30 Mins.

Directions:

1. In your Slow Cooker, mix 2 C. water with salt, pepper, onion, garlic, chipotle powder, chili powder, cumin and pork, stir, cover the Slow Cooker and cook on Low for 7 hours.
2. Transfer meat to a cutting board, shred it with2 forks, add to a bowl, mix with 1 tbsp. of cooking liquid, more salt and pepper, stir and leave aside.
3. In another bowl, mix masa harina with salt, pepper, baking powder, shortening and oil and stir using a mixer.
4. Add cooking liquid from the instant Slow Cooker and blend again well.
5. Unfold corn husks, place them on a work surface, add ¼ C. masa mix near the top of the husk, press into a square and leaves 2 inches at the bottom.
6. Add 1 tbsp. pork mix in the center of the masa, wrap the husk around the dough, place all of them in your Slow Cooker, add the rest of the water, cover and cook on High for 1 hour and 30 minutes.
7. Arrange tamales on a platter and serve.

Tacos

Ingredients:

- 13 oz. canned pinto beans, drained
- ¼ C. chili sauce
- 2 oz. chipotle pepper in adobo sauce, chopped
- ½ tbsp. cocoa powder
- ¼ tsp. cinnamon powder
- 4 taco shells

Servings: 2
Cooking Time: 4 Hours

Directions:

1. In your Slow Cooker, mix the beans with the chili sauce and the other ingredients except the taco shells, toss, put the lid on and cook on Low for 4 hours.
2. Divide the mix into the taco shells and serve them as an appetizer.

Tomato And Mushroom Salsa

Ingredients:

- 1 C. cherry tomatoes, halved
- 1 C. mushrooms, sliced
- 1 small yellow onion, chopped
- 1 garlic clove, minced
- 12 oz. tomato sauce
- ¼ C. cream cheese, cubed
- 1 tbsp. chives, chopped
- Salt and black pepper to the taste

Servings: 2
Cooking Time: 4 Hours

Directions:

1. In your Slow Cooker, mix the tomatoes with the mushrooms and the other ingredients, toss, put the lid on and cook on Low for 4 hours.
2. Divide into bowls and serve as a party salsa

Spinach Mussels Salad

Ingredients:

- 2 lbs. mussels, cleaned and scrubbed
- 1 radicchio, cut into thin strips
- 1 white onion, chopped
- 1 lb. baby spinach
- ½ C. dry white wine
- 1 garlic clove, crushed
- ½ C. of water
- A drizzle of olive oil

Servings: 4
Cooking Time: 1 Hour

Directions:

1. Add mussels, onion, water, oil, garlic, and wine to the Slow Cooker.
2. Put the cooker's lid on and set the cooking time to 1 hour on High settings.
3. Spread the radicchio and spinach in the serving plates.
4. Divide the cooked mussels over the spinach leaves.
5. Serve.

Bacon Fingerling Potatoes

Ingredients:

- 2 lb. fingerling potatoes
- 8 oz. bacon
- 1 tsp onion powder
- 1 tsp chili powder
- 1 tsp garlic powder
- 1 tsp paprika
- 3 tbsp butter
- 1 tsp dried dill
- 1 tbsp rosemary

Servings: 15

Cooking Time: 8 Hours

Directions:

1. Grease the base of your Slow Cooker with butter.
2. Spread the fingerling potatoes in the buttered cooker.
3. Mix all the spices, herbs, and bacon in a bowl.
4. Spread bacon-spice mixture over the lingering potatoes.
5. Put the cooker's lid on and set the cooking time to 8 hours on Low settings.
6. Serve warm.

Eggplant Dip

Ingredients:

- 1 eggplant
- 1 zucchini, chopped
- 2 tbsp. olive oil
- 2 tbsp. balsamic vinegar
- 1 tbsp. parsley, chopped
- 1 yellow onion, chopped
- 1 celery stick, chopped
- 1 tomato, chopped
- 2 tbsp. tomato paste
- 1 and ½ tsp. garlic, minced
- A pinch of sea salt
- Black pepper to the taste

Servings: 4

Cooking Time: 4 Hours And 10 Mins.

Directions:

1. Brush eggplant with the oil, place on preheated grill and cook over medium-high heat for 5 minutes on each side.
2. Leave aside to cool down, chop it and put in your Slow Cooker.
3. Also add, zucchini, vinegar, onion, celery, tomato, parsley, tomato paste, garlic, salt and pepper and stir everything.
4. Cover and cook on High for 4 hours.
5. Stir your spread again very well, divide into bowls and serve.

SIDE DISH
RECIPES

Nut And Berry Side Salad

Ingredients:

- 2 C. strawberries, halved
- 2 tbsp. mint, chopped
- 1/3 C. raspberry vinegar
- 2 tbsp. honey
- 1 tbsp. canola oil
- Salt and black pepper to the taste
- 4 C. spinach, torn
- ½ C. blueberries
- ¼ C. walnuts, chopped
- 1 oz. goat cheese, crumbled

Servings: 4
Cooking Time: 1 Hour

Directions:

1. In your Slow Cooker, mix strawberries with mint, vinegar, honey, oil, salt, pepper, spinach, blueberries and walnuts, cover and cook on High for 1 hour.
2. Divide salad on plates, sprinkle cheese on top and serve as a side dish.

Carrot And Beet Side Salad

Ingredients:

- ½ C. walnuts, chopped
- ¼ C. lemon juice
- ½ C. olive oil
- 1 shallot, chopped
- 1 tsp. Dijon mustard
- 1 tbsp. brown sugar
- Salt and black pepper to the taste
- 2 beets, peeled and cut into wedges
- 2 carrots, peeled and sliced
- 1 C. parsley
- 5 oz. arugula

Servings: 6

Cooking Time: 7 Hours

Directions:

1. In your Slow Cooker, mix beets with carrots, salt, pepper, sugar, mustard, shallot, oil, lemon juice and walnuts, cover and cook on Low for 7 hours.
2. Transfer everything to a bowl, add parsley and arugula, toss, divide between plates and serve as a side dish.

Cauliflower Pilaf

Ingredients:

- 1 C. cauliflower rice
- 6 green onions, chopped
- 3 tbsp. ghee, melted
- 2 garlic cloves, minced
- ½ lb. Portobello mushrooms, sliced
- 2 C. warm water
- Salt and black pepper to the taste

Servings: 6
Cooking Time: 3 Hours

Directions:

1. In your Slow Cooker, mix cauliflower rice with green onions, melted ghee, garlic, mushrooms, water, salt and pepper, stir well, cover and cook on Low for 3 hours.
2. Divide between plates and serve as a side dish.

Buttery Artichokes

Ingredients:

- 13 oz. artichoke heart halved
- 1 tsp salt
- 4 C. chicken stock
- 1 tsp turmeric
- 1 garlic clove, peeled
- 4 tbsp butter
- 4 oz. Parmesan, shredded

Servings: 5
Cooking Time: 6 Hrs.

Directions:

1. Add artichoke, stock, salt, and turmeric to the Slow Cooker.
2. Put the cooker's lid on and set the cooking time to 6 hours on Low settings.
3. Drain and transfer the cooked artichoke to the serving plates.
4. Drizzle, cheese, and butter over the artichoke.
5. Serve warm.

Tamale Side Dish

Ingredients:

- 12 oz. masa harina
- 1 C. chicken stock
- ½ tsp salt
- 1 tsp onion powder
- 1 onion, chopped
- 5 tbsp olive oil
- 5 corn husks
- 5 C. of water

Servings: 5
Cooking Time: 7 Hours

Directions:

1. Chicken Mix masa harina with chicken salt, salt, onion powder.
2. Stir in the chopped onion, and olive oil, then knead this dough.
3. Soak corn husks for 15 minutes in water then drain.
4. Spread the corn husks on the working surface.
5. Divide the masa harina mixture over the corn husks.
6. Roll the corn husk around the filling, then place these rolls in the Slow Cooker.
7. Put the cooker's lid on and set the cooking time to 7 hours on Low settings.
8. Serve fresh.

Herbed Balsamic Beets

Ingredients:

- 6 medium assorted-color beets, peeled and cut into wedges
- 2 tbsp balsamic vinegar
- 2 tbsp olive oil
- 2 tbsp chives, chopped
- 1 tbsp tarragon, chopped
- Salt and black pepper to the taste
- 1 tsp orange peel, grated

Servings: 4

Cooking Time: 7 Hours

Directions:

1. Add beets, tarragon, and rest of the ingredients to the Slow Cooker.
2. Put the cooker's lid on and set the cooking time to 7 hours on Low settings.
3. Serve warm.

Ramen Noodles

Ingredients:

- 1 tbsp ramen seasoning
- 10 oz. ramen noodles
- 4 C. chicken stock
- 1 tsp salt
- 3 tbsp soy sauce
- 1 tsp paprika
- 1 tbsp butter

Servings: 5

Cooking Time: 25 Mins.

Directions:

1. Add chicken stock, butter, ramen, paprika, noodles and all other ingredients to the Slow Cooker.
2. Put the cooker's lid on and set the cooking time to 25 minutes on High settings.
3. Serve warm.

Cinnamon Applesauce

Ingredients:

- 1 lb. red apples, peeled and chopped
- 2 oz. cinnamon stick
- 1 tsp ground ginger
- ½ tsp nutmeg
- 1 tsp ground cinnamon
- 4 oz. water
- ½ tsp salt
- 1 tbsp lime juice

Servings: 5
Cooking Time: 6 Hrs.

Directions:

1. Add red apples, cinnamon stick, salt, cinnamon ground, water, lime juice, nutmeg, and ginger to the Slow Cooker.
2. Put the cooker's lid on and set the cooking time to 6 hours on High settings.
3. Discard the cinnamon sticks from the apples.
4. Serve fresh.
5. Transfer the dish to the serving bowls and serve it or keep in the fridge for not more than 3 days. Enjoy!

VEGETABLE & VEGETARIAN RECIPES

Chorizo Cashew Salad

Ingredients:

- 8 oz. chorizo, chopped
- 1 tsp olive oil
- 1 tsp cayenne pepper
- 1 tsp chili flakes
- 1 tsp ground black pepper
- 1 tsp onion powder
- 2 garlic cloves
- 3 tomatoes, chopped
- 1 C. lettuce, torn
- 1 C. fresh dill
- 1 tsp oregano
- 3 tbsp crushed cashews

Servings: 6
Cooking Time: 4 Hours 30 Mins.

Directions:

1. Add chorizo sausage to the Slow Cooker.
2. Put the cooker's lid on and set the cooking time to 4 hours on High settings.
3. Mix chili flakes, cayenne pepper, black pepper, and onion powder in a bowl.
4. Now add tomatoes to the Slow Cooker and cover again.
5. Slow Cooker for another 30 minutes on High setting.
6. Stir in oregano and dill then mix well.
7. Add sliced garlic and torn lettuce to the mixture.
8. Garnish with cashews.
9. Serve.

Eggplant Parmesan Casserole

Ingredients:

- 1 medium eggplant, sliced
- 1 large egg
- Salt and pepper to taste
- 1 C. almond flour
- 1 C. parmesan cheese

Servings: 3
Cooking Time: 3 Hours

Directions:

1. Place the eggplant slices in the Slow Cooker.
2. Pour in the eggs and season with salt and pepper.
3. Stir in the almond flour and sprinkle with parmesan cheese.
4. Stir to combine everything.
5. Close the lid and cook on low for 3 hours or on high for 2 hours.

Walnut Kale

Ingredients:

- 5 C. kale, chopped
- 2 oz walnuts, chopped
- 1 C. of coconut milk
- 1 tsp. vegan butter
- 1 C. of water
- 1 oz vegan Parmesan, grated

Servings: 4
Cooking Time: 5 Hours

Directions:

1. Put all ingredients in the Slow Cooker and gently stir.
2. Then close the lid and cook the kale on Low for 5 hours.

Eggplant Mini Wraps

Ingredients:

- 10 oz. eggplant, sliced into rounds
- 5 oz. halloumi cheese
- 1 tsp minced garlic
- 3 oz. bacon, chopped
- ½ tsp ground black pepper
- 1 tsp salt
- 1 tsp paprika
- 1 tomato

Servings: 6

Cooking Time: 5 Hrs

Directions:

1. Season the eggplant sliced with salt, paprika, and black pepper.
2. Add these slices to the Slow Cooker and spread in a single layer.
3. Put the cooker's lid on and set the cooking time to 1 hour on High settings.
4. Allow the eggplant to cool then top them with tomato and cheese slices.
5. And top them with bacon and garlic.
6. Roll each slice and insert the toothpick to seal them.
7. Place these wrap in the Slow Cooker carefully.
8. Put the cooker's lid on and set the cooking time to 4 hours on High settings.
9. Serve fresh.

Rainbow Bake

Ingredients:

- 1 zucchini, sliced
- 1 tomato, sliced
- 1 eggplant, sliced
- 1 red onion, sliced
- 1 tbsp. coconut oil
- 1 tsp. salt
- 1 tsp. dried parsley
- 1 tsp. chili powder
- 1 C. of water

Servings: 4

Cooking Time: 6 Hours

Directions:

1. Carefully grease the Slow Cooker bowl with coconut oil.
2. Then put zucchini, tomato, eggplant, and onion in the Slow Cooker one-by-one.
3. Sprinkle the vegetables with salt, dried parsley, and chili powder.
4. Add water and close the lid.
5. Cook the meal on Low for 6 hours.

Tofu Kebabs

Ingredients:

- 2 tbsp. lemon juice
- 1 tsp. ground turmeric
- 2 tbsp. coconut cream
- 1 tsp. chili powder
- ¼ C. of water
- 1 tsp. avocado oil
- 1-lb. tofu, cubed

Servings: 4

Cooking Time: 2 Hours

Directions:

1. Pour water in the Slow Cooker.
2. After this, in the mixing bowl mix lemon juice, ground turmeric, coconut cream, chili powder, and avocado oil.
3. Coat every tofu cube in the coconut cream mixture and string on the wooden skewers. Place them in the Slow Cooker.
4. Cook the tofu kebabs on Low for 2 hours.

Zucchini Basil Soup

Ingredients:

- 9 C. zucchini, diced
- 2 C. white onions, chopped
- 4 C. vegetable broth
- 8 cloves of garlic, minced
- 1 C. basil leaves
- 4 tbsp. olive oil
- Salt and pepper to taste

Servings: 8
Cooking Time: 3 Hours

Directions:

1. Place the ingredients in the Slow Cooker.
2. Give a good stir.
3. Close the lid and cook on high for 2 hours or on low for 3 hours.
4. Once cooked, transfer into a blender and pulse until smooth.

Brussel Sprouts

Ingredients:

- 1-lb. Brussel sprouts
- 2 oz tofu, chopped, cooked
- 1 tsp. cayenne pepper
- 2 C. of water
- 1 tbsp. vegan butter

Servings: 4
Cooking Time: 2.5 Hours

Directions:

1. Pour water in the Slow Cooker.
2. Add Brussel sprouts and cayenne pepper.
3. Cook the vegetables on high for 2.5 hours.
4. Then drain water and mix Brussel sprouts with butter and tofu.
5. Shake the vegetables gently.

OTHER SLOW COOKER RECIPES

Beans With Bacon

Ingredients:

- 3 (16-ounce) cans baked beans
- 6 strips bacon, cut in 1-inch pieces
- ¼ C. brown sugar, packed
- ½ C. ketchup
- ½ tsp. mustard powder

Directions:

1. Fry the bacon until it is brown and crispy.
2. Pour the beans into the Slow Cooker and add the bacon.
3. Mix together brown sugar, mustard powder and ketchup in a bowl.
4. Pour this mixture into the Slow Cooker and cover the lid.
5. Cook on HIGH for about 2 hours and dish out to serve hot.

Vegetarian Spanish Rice

Servings: 3

Cooking Time: 6 Hours 10 Mins.

Ingredients:

- 1 C. rice
- 1 C. vegetable broth
- ½ (15 ounce) can diced tomatoes
- ½ onion, diced
- ½ green bell pepper, diced
- 1 tsp. chili powder
- 1/8 C. salsa
- ¾ tsp. garlic powder
- ½ tsp. onion powder

Directions:

1. Place the rice in the Slow Cooker and top with the remaining ingredients.
2. Cover the lid and cook for about 6 hours on LOW.
3. Dish out and serve hot.

Vegetable Rice

Ingredients:

- ¼ C. sun-dried tomato, finely chopped
- 1 tbsp. lemon juice
- 1 C. rice
- ½ large onion, sliced
- 1 pinch ground turmeric
- ½ C. roasted red pepper, chopped
- 2 garlic cloves, minced
- ¼ tsp. salt
- ¼ C. green pepper, finely diced
- 1 stalk celery, sliced
- 1 carrot, sliced
- ¼ tsp. black pepper
- 1 tbsp. fresh parsley, minced
- 2 C. vegetable stock
- ½ tbsp. extra-virgin olive oil
- ¾ C. frozen peas

Servings: 3
Cooking Time: 4 Hours 45 Mins.

Directions:

1. Heat oil in a large skillet and add carrots, onions, garlic and celery.
2. Sauté for about 4 minutes and transfer into the Slow Cooker.
3. Add rice, sun-dried tomatoes, saffron, vegetable stock, salt and black pepper.
4. Cover and cook for about 4 hours on LOW.
5. Stir in the green pepper, peas, lemon juice and red pepper.
6. Cover and cook for about 20 minutes on HIGH.
7. Garnish with parsley to serve hot.

Slow Cooker Pinto Beans

Ingredients:

- 2 tsp. extra-virgin olive oil
- 1½ tsp. kosher salt, divided
- 2 C. pinto beans, rinsed
- 1 small yellow onion, diced
- 1 jalapeno, cored, seeded and finely chopped
- 3 garlic cloves, minced
- 1 tsp. ground cumin
- ¼ tsp. cayenne pepper
- 4 C. low-sodium chicken broth
- 2 bay leaves
- 1 tsp. dried oregano
- 3 C. water

Servings: 6
Cooking Time: 8 Hours 20 Mins.

Directions:

1. Place the pinto beans in the Slow Cooker and keep aside.
2. Heat the oil in a skillet over a medium-high heat and add onions, garlic and jalapeno.
3. Sauté for about 3 minutes and transfer to the Slow Cooker along with the bay leaves, oregano, cumin, cayenne and salt.
4. Top with broth and water and cover the lid.
5. Cook on HIGH for about 8 hours and dish out to serve hot.

Moroccan Beef Rice

Ingredients:

- 1 lb. boneless beef, cut into 1-inch pieces
- 1 small apple, shredded
- 1 (6.9-oz.) package rice and vermicelli mix with chicken seasonings
- ¼ C. almonds, slivered
- ¼ C. raisins
- 1 tsp. curry powder
- 1½ C. chicken broth

Servings: 4
Cooking Time: 9 Hours 20 Mins.

Directions:

1. Mix together beef, curry powder, apple, broth and seasoning packet from rice mix in a Slow Cooker.
2. Cover the lid and cook for about 8 hours 30 minutes on LOW.
3. Uncover and add rice, raisins and almonds.
4. Cover the lid and cook for about 30 minutes on HIGH.
5. Dish out to serve hot.

Mexican Bean Stew

Ingredients:

- 1 (7.5 oz) can chopped tomatoes with green chilies
- ½ C. brown rice
- 1 C. water
- 1 (7.5 oz) can chili beans
- 1 (7.5 oz) can sweet corn
- 1 (7.5 oz) can butter beans
- ½ packet taco meat seasoning

Servings: 5

Cooking Time: 4 Hours 10 Mins.

Directions:

1. Put all the ingredients in the Slow Cooker and mix well.
2. Cover and cook on LOW for about 4 hours.
3. Dish out in a bowl and serve hot.

Coconut Rice

Ingredients:

- 4½ C. water
- 2 C. lengthy grain white rice
- 4 tbsp. butter
- 1 C. unsweetened coconut, grated
- 1 tsp. salt
- 1 C. fresh parsley
- 1 tsp. cinnamon powder

Servings: 6

Cooking Time: 3 Hours 45 Mins.

Directions:

1. Put butter and rice in the Slow Cooker and cook on HIGH for about 15 minutes.
2. Add the remaining ingredients and cover the lid.
3. Cook for about 3 hours 30 minutes on LOW and dish out to serve.

Slow Cooker Beef Biryani

Ingredients:

- 1 tsp. garam masala
- 2 lb. stewing beef
- 1 tsp. ground coriander
- ½ C. natural yogurt
- 1 knob ginger, grated
- 1 bunch coriander
- 1 tsp. ground turmeric
- 1 tsp. chili powder
- 1 tbsp. olive oil
- 2 cinnamon quills
- 2 C. basmati rice
- 4 garlic cloves, grated
- 4 onions, sliced
- 3 C. beef stock

Servings: 6

Cooking Time: 4 Hours 15 Mins

Directions:

1. Mix together yogurt, coriander, ginger, garlic and spices in a bowl.
2. Stir in the beef to mix well and transfer into the Slow Cooker and top with rice.
3. Sauté onions in oil for about 3 minutes and layer over the rice.
4. Pour in stock and cinnamon quills and cover the lid.
5. Cook on HIGH for about 4 hours.
6. Top with additional coriander leaves and serve hot.

Milton Keynes UK
Ingram Content Group UK Ltd.
UKHW051120241023
431235UK00012B/357

9 781804 462133